T0197140

IF I HAD KNOWN...

JOCELYN SWANSON

authorHOUSE

AuthorHouse™
1663 Liberty Drive
Bloomington, IN 47403
www.authorhouse.com
Phone: 833-262-8899

Published by AuthorHouse 11/08/2022

ISBN: 978-1-6655-7428-0 (sc)
ISBN: 978-1-6655-7427-3 (hc)
ISBN: 978-1-6655-7447-1 (e)

Library of Congress Control Number: 2022919974

Contents

Awareness and Grief.. 1

Family.. 27

Health.. 49

Education.. 59

Relationship 85

Faith 97

Finances 127

Time 139

Choices 145

Foreword

IF I Had Known

No matter what your age, gender race or profession, have you ever thought or uttered the words, "If I had known…"? Sure, you have, but sometimes the simplest words or thoughts can become the seeds of something great, something that can serve as the basis for helping others. At least that is what happens to me.

One morning I was listening to my own spirit and these words echoed, resonated and were repeated: "If I had known/ If I had known…" I meditated on that phrase and realized that it could have been very possible that someone else, at that very moment, may well have been thinking the same exact thing. I decided to act on my impulses.

I called all my friends who had children in college, about to go to college, or knew someone with young people in that age group. I had an idea about this particular set of young people because them to have the benefit of wisdom and retrospect; why can't they have the benefit of what we have learned and in doing so, avoid the problems, pitfalls, and obstacles that might stand in their way? It was simple:

I wanted young people to have options, confidence, and to know how to network and live their dreams. A great person once said that having options in life is what freedom really is. It was based on these thoughts and the notes that I jotted down following these brainstorms that IF I Had Known took root as a mentoring program for young people.

To begin this journey, I contacted (8) professional women, including doctors, lawyer, social workers, pharmacist, teacher, nurse, and a medical technologist. When we got together, I asked them to share with the group what they "wished they had known" and how having that kind of knowledge, before embarking on a college life, their chosen vocation, or even marriage – how knowing ahead of time could have perhaps made their paths and transitions easier and smoother.

Acknowledgments

I want to thank God for the vision for this book and for the provision to get it published.

To my brilliant, amazing, and handsome husband, I just want to thank you for believing in my every dream and goal and giving me the support, I needed to achieve this goal. You are my best friend and the best husband. I am blessed to have found you.

To my son John, you were a gift from God, we've been through a lot as mother and son. A lot we both wish we had known. Lessons learned and Faith increased for us both. I am very proud of you for being obedient and most of all for your unconditional love.

To Jennifer, thank you for your love, and our beautiful granddaughters. Ava, I see you blooming like a flower you are beautiful and smart, I am honored to be a part of your life. Harlowe you are our little energy bundle of joy. Like your big sis, you're beautiful, smart and keeps us laughing and amazed.

To Chip (Kaylee) and Alison (Kevin) thank you for Milo, Jett, Kevin and Caleb the sweetest most handsome, and talented little boys and young men. I am thankful that I could be on your family tree.

To my brothers Duane and Bertrand, I love you so much. Thank you for always loving me and being there for me. Franklin showed me how to believe in myself. Johnetta taught me how to appreciate the art of music. I miss you both but will always remember your lessons to pass on.

Special thanks to Jessica Debnam for always helping me with all the If I had known projects. Kaleb Lathan & Linda Robbins for all your help with starting the process. Jamila Thomas for your referral to the talented Cameron Wilson (illustrator).

To all of you that took the time to participate in my project and give your wisdom and hard knock lessons. I thank you so very much. I know this will give someone the wisdom and the confidence they need.

Just a few words:

This book or this question is not to say you would ever want your life to change, although some do say their path would have gone a different way, mostly for the good. We all know the valleys; the struggles and the heartaches make us strong and defines the person we become. There are so many times we wish someone had just told us a few words of wisdom or the lessons they learned. Sometimes it is because certain people aren't in our lives or taken out of our lives, sometimes it is no fault of ours.

Sometimes it is because we didn't ask, we didn't know to ask, or what to ask or too afraid to ask.

I wish I had known that I didn't have to be afraid to talk to people, most people want to talk they're quite curious about you just as you are about them. They want to talk about their animals, kids, husband, friends, what they like and don't like and life.

This pandemic made us all aware of how much we want and need to talk to each other. Some of us we wish we had known, we had so little time to ask the questions we wanted to know.

I want to thank all of you that grasped the vision of what was trying to be accomplished with this book and took the time to share your story. I do understand, obstacles make us who we are. I wanted to help a young person or a person no matter who, what age they are to have hope and know that no matter what the obstacle, they can overcome it and turn themselves around.

Chapter

Awareness
and Grief

Zenetta S Drew

I saw Ms. Drew on August 8, 2014. Ms. Drew was the guest speaker for the graduating class. At that time Ms. Drew was the Executive Director of the Dallas Black Dance Company, Ms. Drew is poise elegant and tenacious. The opening words of Ms. Drew's speech was "let me tell you what I wish I had known" I was captured and all eyes forward. I looked for Ms. Drew afterwards because I had just said that morning, I wanted to do a book titled If I had known, I knew she got what I was saying and thinking what I was trying to convey to the people that would read this book. I called and left a message and after a few days, a Thursday to be exact, I received a call back and was graced with an appointment. Not only that, but I visited with Ms. Drew and just as on August 8, I was again captivated by the words and wisdom of Ms. Drew.

I ask her what she wished she had known, and she said there were many.

The one that was so important to me, and I feel a lot of people would benefit from what she wishes she had known, she wishes that she had listened to people's No's. No has benefits that can help you get your next yes. You need to understand why people are saying no because the next person you talk to, you can avoid the mistake you made with the first. You don't have to agree with them, and they don't have to agree with you.

Chad

I met Chad at a class at the Plano center, he was teaching how
to write our life story. He was very patience and knowledgeable
and I knew any book I pursued I would contact him for
guidance. I asked him what his If I had known was, and he
explained, growing up in Tokyo, he wishes he would have
learned the Japanese language. I would have been able to work
there and raise my family there.

Maryland

I wish I had known not to grow up so fast, that life has a lot to offer if you take it day by day.

Jarvis

I wish I had known that what my mother was telling me was right at 23 years old. She told me about life and women. My mother was very tough, well at least that was what I thought, she was just getting me ready for life. She did let me know that as a man your name should mean something.

I do wish I had known about credit, but our parents didn't do credit, so no lessons were taught about it, but she did teach me how to pay bills.

Edid

Born in Puerto Rico and raised in Spain, came here by accident, and just thought he would only visit for vacation. He wanted to be an oral Surgeon, but an accident caused him to redirect his decision, he was hit in the eye by a wind mass and was told he would not be able to see small things. This did not keep him from achieving his dreams or goals, they were adjusted a little, but he still went to medical school, taught in San Antonio, and later opened his own practice.

When ask what you wish you had known, he said I wish I had known whatever seems easy is going to be the hardest.

Matthew

Matthew is a research coordinator loves his job and wishes he had known, a lot earlier, to enjoy life day by day and what's given to you.

Growing up in Indonesia, Matthew wishes he had known to enjoy the culture and appreciate the community love and the food.

Lithuania

I wish I had known more about the American Culture. When I got here in the states, I was like a little fish in a big pond.

Mariesa

Mariesa is a family friend beautiful inside and out, she and her brother Jordon have a very caring and loving relationship for family.

I wish I would have known not to stress out about setbacks, rather focus more on framing them as learning opportunities or steppingstones. It would have allowed me to spend more time constructively reflecting and be more giving of my time and energy to others and staying focused on the big picture while fully enjoying little moments. This would have allowed me to emit more positive energy to those who spent emotional energy consoling me or encouraging me.

Peru

Glenda is an intern and will become a great doctor because of her outlook on life. When I met her, she had been in Dallas only three weeks.

Glenda stated coming up, the schooling is a little different from what I know. You make up your mind early as to what you want to become, seems as though you must stay focus not just starting your freshman year in high school, but all the way through.

I had a moment when I just wanted to quit, but I started to look at life differently. She wish she had known earlier that there has to be a balance of family, friends as well as the studies to complete you and conquer your goals.

If you feel good about yourself, you'll do good for others, she says.

New Jersey

I wish I had known that my generation was vastly different from my parents. They met in college got their masters, married, house and kids by the age of 26. The men and women of my generation are so self-centered, self-pleasing. They aren't mature, or desire marriage or hold down a stable job until they are 40 years old.

Resident2

I wish I had known before you make a career decision, to understand how and if your professional duties align with your own moral beliefs, not only for your first job but for the position that you aspire to hold in the future.

Shemika

Shemika is on her way to becoming a dental hygienist and loves to help keep teeth straight for a confident smile and person.

When ask what she wish she had known, these were her words:

If I had known that I didn't have to settle for less and didn't have to have the feeling of insecurity, I could have been where I am now and further. I wish I had known I wasn't alone, and I had everything I needed to be what I wanted and dreamed of doing.

I love my children and they are God's gift to me, but I would not have had children before marriage, I would have given them what they deserved. Furthermore, I would have loved myself more and this would have guided me to stay focus on what I really wanted to do in my life. I would have been emotionally healed, and not broken, most of all I would have been closer to God.

Syed

I wish I had known my personality profile; it would have helped me understand myself and why I do certain things. I am starting to use this knowledge in emotional intelligence.

Syria

I wish I had known I loved linguistics, I am just now discovering the interest I have in languages and the meaning of the same words in different countries and cultures. My life could have been different if I had known.

Avant

This question brought a smile to this military man's face retired Master Sargent Avant, he proceeded to continue the conversation with If I had known to use the resources available to me to save and invest money at an early age, I would have been in a better financial place now. I wish I had known to be an employer instead of an employee.

1% of 99 people is better than 100% of yourself because everyone has something important to offer.

Eugene

I wish I had known it was ok to talk to people. Growing up I was shy, and I would say protected by my parents. I didn't know what to say, thinking what I wanted to talk about was not what anyone else wanted to talk about. I found out that if I had to talk to people, the more you find out about them and find out about information that could benefit you.

The irony is I ended up becoming a psychiatrist, so I talk to people all the time now.

Dr. Allen

As I talked to this doctor of psychiatry, it made me realize how normal it is to make a mistake and how important not to think anyone doesn't make mistakes.

I asked him what he wish he had known, and he said he wishes he had known it was alright to make mistakes. As I went through my rotations in medical school and became increasingly interested in psychiatry, I found out that no one is perfect. I had been a perfectionist all my life, so I thought.

Uganda

I wish I had known I would have been coming to America. Things would have been a little different. Starting from food, living, particularly employment and language or accent.

On my arrival, I would say different things in a British accent where no one could understand me. The jobs I wanted to pursue here; I was forced to go back to school since I had to meet the American Standards. I wish I had known how to prepare, and life would have been easier the first year I arrived in America from Uganda.

Eric

I wish I had known that Earth is 93 million miles from the Sun, the center of our solar system, which is not the center of our galaxy, which if we traveled inside a spaceship moving at 10 miles per second would take us nearly 2 billion years to fly across. Our Sun is one of hundreds of billions of stars in our galaxy, which is one of 2 trillion galaxies in the observable Universe, the nearest one to ours being 2.5 million light years away. The Universe, which is 13.8 billion years old and continues to expand, contains the Sun, which is 4.5 billion years old and halfway through its lifecycle, around which orbits the Earth, on which live 7.8 billion humans who have existed only 200,000 years. Even if I am "one in a million", this means there are 7,800 people exactly like me, just on one planet in one of 2 trillion galaxies in one of millions of galaxy super clusters in only one ever-expanding, observable Universe.

If I had known this earlier, I would have realized that I am an infinitesimally small part of a much bigger design, and there is much I don't know or understand about my place. I would have focused more on my contribution to a greater utility, and less on achievement or outside recognition. I would have learned to stay in the present more and not worry about things out of my control. I would have prioritized relationships over accolades. I would have laughed at my mistakes. Most importantly, I would have learned to accept failure for nothing more than growing into the best version of myself.

Latifah

When ask this question "What do you wish you had known" it really challenges your mind. That's what happened in this case. Latifah, was ask the question by Tabitha and was eager to have her share her story. Latifah was happy to give her wisdom to help someone else.

I wish I had known to wait to get married and went to school to do what I wanted to do. I could have finished my degrees and reached my goals. My marriage slowed me down, with me being married it was always a "we" thing. The system would always want "our" information. It was hard for me to shine and help make our life better. It was always me never "us" I wasted my years of being married when I could have done a lot. I felt as if my husband was holding me back from a lot. If I had stayed single a while longer, I would have accomplished my dreams by now. I wasn't ready for marriage, so if I had waited, I would have matured more and knew exactly what I wanted.

Pastor

I met this man at work as I was talking to him, he told me he was also a pastor. I ask him what did he wish he had known? He immediately said, I wish I had known the pain of losing a son. I had a moment of silence; I could see the pain in his eyes and on his face.

Most of us have suffered a lost in our families or friendships. We are never ready for the lost, hurt or the pain and even when we know the end is coming for our loved ones, we wish we had known how to handle it.

Chapter

Family

Fatima

I met Fatima in a class at Texas A&M-Commerce, we were assigned to do a project together, when I found out she wanted to do the assignment ahead of time I was ecstatic. That was all I knew about Fatima; she was timely and smart. I have recently learned more about her story and understand why she is extremely focused. Fatima was a teenage mom and says what she wishes she had known was why I shouldn't have had a baby at such a young age, it would have been a great help to me. Of course, she was told don't get pregnant, but the explanation of finances, how much it cost to raise a child and, in my case, a special needs child and emotional stress I would encounter. Fatima is to be commended for her determination to be a great mother, and social worker she is now a Clinical Social worker.

Stuart

I was entertained by Stuart's sign on the streets of New York City, it read "I Need money for weed". Stuart is originally from South Philadelphia came to New York to do something different, to be a street performer, do some acting and become famous. I wanted to explore everything, I wanted to make people laugh I knew if I did that, I knew I was doing something right. I felt, no matter what other people thought of me, I was doing what I was put here to do. If I had known I was going to do this, I would have done it a long time ago. It is different, and I want to be different and not have a conventional job as others. I choose to be in the entertainment business it is hard, and I don't blame others for not trying this because it is not easy to work, and not get recognition for it. I meet people from all over the world every day I hear their amazing stories of their life struggles and what they go through, and I learn from them, and they learn from me.

I have done construction work behind the desk working with people, but I did not find it as fulfilling as I do with this job now for the last four years. Many people don't like what my sign says. Most people give me money they get a kick out of my sign, and it makes them laugh.

Joann

I met Joann in line to buy tickets to the Rockets performance, we immediately started up a conversation. My first question was could we go for coffee and discuss what you wish you had known, she gladly agreed, learning about Joann was interesting. She was born in China and now lives in New Zealand. She was an assistant teacher, but her parents were not please with that career.

Joann wishes she had known that spending more time with her daughter was more important than making money.

Joann moved to Shenzhen to make money in import export business to send her daughter to St. Cuthbert. My parents fostered my daughter. I think my relationship would be different with my daughter if I had been with her more, I do feel guilty of not spending time with her. Joann said kids should be looked after by their parents, not completely by the grandparents.

I just wish I had known to be a mother.

Kentucky

I wish I would have known to appreciate my mother more. I wish I had known how much she did for me and how much she loved me.

Stephanie

I wish I had known what my parents were experiencing. When I became a parent, I did understand, and I would have acted differently, but my realization and actions were too late.

Laquered

Petite and full of life, Laquered a navy veteran loves her dog and is proud of her service in the Navy.

Laquered answered the question If I had known, I would have stayed in the Navy and traveled the world if I had known I wasn't going to have children.

Jovan

We all have a story whether we want to let others know is up to us, Jovan was nice enough to let be in on his If I had known story. He started out by saying it is not a sad story, it's a true story. My father killed my mother. Jovon was born 1980. He was raised by different relatives in different states, he lived in the Bronx, Brooklyn, Harlem. He was an only child and says he was exposed to things that he shouldn't have, but because there was no mother there to hold your hand and tell you what to do and what not to do. I used to be a kleptomaniac, steal lie, but I learned that was evil, and you can't pay me to do that now.

My grandmother promised me that if I came to live with her, I would have all my needs met, and she would save money for me to go to college. That didn't happen, just the opposite. Deceive by my relatives because of a check.

I now wish I had known my parents to get the unconditional love, guidance, and the wisdom that parents, teach you as a child and even when you are an adult. Even if it is not your parents, you need a positive influence to help you through this journey of life. Like Whitney Houston use to sing, I believe the children are our future, teach them well and let them lead the way.

Michael

Sometimes when you're listening to people stories, you can't help but become emotional, even though you try not to do so right there in front of them. But at the same time these are human beings and when it deals with childhood, I become very empathetic. Even though Michael is an adult with a son of his, own. It was painful, but admirable that he never gave up in being a good person, a helping person.

Michael is now a social worker, but this young man's journey to this goal wasn't easy. The fact of the matter is, his end result may not have happened if his childhood had been an easy one.

To say that Michael had a negative family life would be a major understatement.

Michael felt as though he was the scapegoat of the family, his mother treated him differently. In his mother's eyes, he recalls, he was and would be the least likely to succeed, she felt he was unattractive, untalented, darker skinned. Furthermore, he claims to have been the child that did and was punished for everything wrong.

Michael knew from this experience he wanted to help people, this gave him the passion to help unwanted, and people that are struggling through life emotionally.

Michael's If I had known moment was when he once said to himself, "I wish I had known everything was going to work out. If I did, I would not have spent so much time lamenting my situation or torturing myself. But one thing about it, I know that God would send someone to love me despite my childhood.

And that is what happened. Michael met a young woman who had faith in him, adored him and helped him get through his malaise.

Lee

There's always a question that gets right to the heart of a person's life, good or bad; this one struck right through the heart. When ask what you wish you had known, the answer was; I wish I had known how unfair the justice system was. I would have never gotten married, nor would I have had children because it hurts not being able to see my kids.

Nigeria

This proud dad to be hails from Nigeria, you could see the joy in his face and eyes when he commented about becoming a father.

When I ask him what he wish he had known, he said I wish I had known to have kids earlier. I wish I had been less selfish; I just wanted it to be all about me. I now know how much I was missing.

Resident

What's important is valuing family and friends. I wish I had known how essential it is to keep up with that part of my life, as well as my books and career.

MD.

Thinking that someone has it all because it looks that way to you on the outside, but there are unfilled dreams that we don't see until we ask. I ask this newly graduated doctor what she wish she had known, and she said I wish I had thought about planning to have kids before I was in medical school.

Dr. Janet

As a child and especially the teenage years, you always think someone is looking at you. If they only knew how much parents love them and want the best for them. I wish I had known that my parents just loved me, they were not trying to be mean. I learned that when I became a parent.

Rhode Island

When ask about Rhode Island, she said I can honestly say no matter wherever you go there you really do run into someone you know.

When ask what she wish she had known, she said I wish I had appreciated where I lived and enjoyed my surroundings.

Cameron

Cameron and I met in San Antonio, where he is the head coach for Trinity University. Cameron is a winning coach for the girls' basketball team.

Cameron

I wish I had known, to outwardly appreciate my parents so much more along the way. The stages we go through as young people are so valuable to our development, but the things we don't know, even as adults, are staggering. My mother and father gave us everything, and my behavior didn't always illustrate how appreciative I should have been. I have learned to express how much I appreciate them as I have grown up. I believe life is about the moments and I wouldn't have missed opportunities to thank them the right way, in the moment, because being a parent now myself, I know how much those moments mean to moms and dads.

I know that I am able to see past the immediate behavior, in the moment and know how much love is in my house. My boys are my whole world, and they know dad is always there for them. I am a better father knowing how much I appreciate what my parents did for me. I may not have always shown how much it really meant to me right then and there. My opportunity is in being the best father and husband I can be, seeing the bigger picture.

I value friendship so much that I only have a handful of Real friends. Understanding how to let people know that they are important to you and that you appreciate them is one of the most meaningful things we can do for each other.

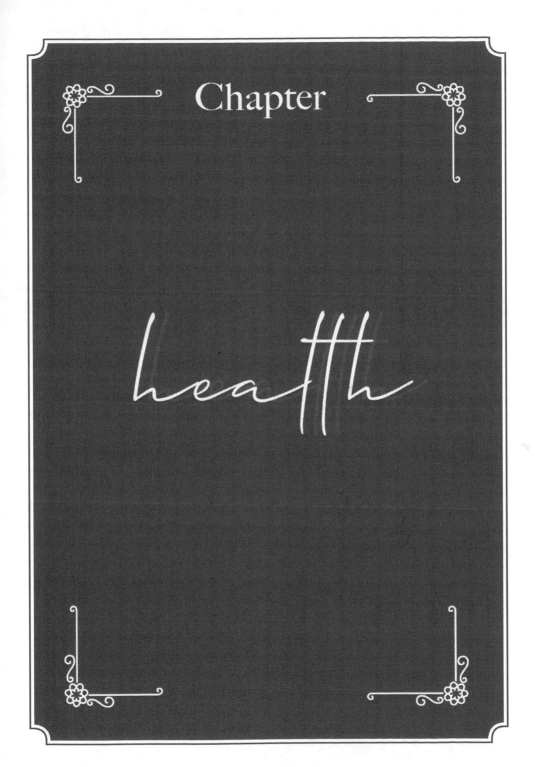

Chapter

health

Shirley Franklin

I was elated to talk to Ms. Franklin as the former Mayor of Atlanta I was sure there were many If I had known moments, and she gave me her best one of all. If you are not in good health and taking time to enjoy family and life you are missing life it self. Ms. Franklin stated, I wish I had known there was a chance of me living until 80 years old. All these revelations came with age, but also being willing to know that if I had known how much information is out there. To know how much technology is available to keep us alive and the knowledge we now have to increase our life span, dental, medical and nutritional. I would have taken a little more time along the way to spend with my children, my grandchildren, my parents. I was so busy rushing to get to 65 or 70. I came to this conclusion by the reflections of my life I missed. I dreamed of taking a month off going somewhere relaxing and spending time with family and friends I didn't do it, and it wasn't that I couldn't do it, I just kept putting it off. People that were there with me shared my concerns, I could have come to these realizations much, much earlier.

It would have given us more time to get to know each other in more than quick events, crisis, or special events, just a normal everyday countryside moment, and days.

I want young people and people in general to know my mother's adage is Stop and Smell the Roses is really true. You must do that in your life every day, every week even in tough times to sustain yourself spiritually and emotionally, you can't wait till you need to pray, or you need to reflect, or you need to relate to folks, you need to stop the rush and enjoy along the way.

Annie

Annie is as wise as she is nice, retaining her smooth skin and beauty. Annie and I met at a pain management group, and I have to say she makes you feel as she has known you forever.

Annie told me she wishes she had known that exercising was such a vital part of your later life. She said she had been very diligent in her earlier years, but it wasn't as important as it should have been, but once you stray away from the routine it is hard to get it back. You become very sedimentary the routine is broken as well as the momentum that you need to fulfil the emotional, physical, and mental health that you acquire from exercise. Annie reiterates that If I had known exercise was so significant, I definitely would have continued and would be in better health now.

Mark

Mark hails from Jamaica, but I met him in Atlanta, I immediately ask what he wish he had known? Well, it didn't take long for a response, it was like he had been pondering this for some time. He gave me this response:

My mother was diagnosed with stage four Metastatic cancer some years ago and shortly after placed on hospice. In talking to one of the doctors caring for her, he shared that the cancer would have been developing in her cells, possibly five or six years before she had the outward signs. He told me that there was one device out there that measures antioxidant levels that could have made us suspicious that something was wrong had she been measuring that level every couple month.

This would have changed my life, because I would have paid more attention to wellness for my entire family, which I do now. I honestly believe that my mother would be alive today had I known what I know now.

This did create a new opportunity for me, I have since started my own wellness business in the hopes of helping the larger community not have a similar situation as I did.

My relationship with my mom was very close, so the only thing that would have changed is getting more time with her.

Bea

Bea is a beautiful Christian woman, I got to really know her and became friends, and now she's more like a sister to me.

I asked her one day did she have an If I had known moment, she said yes a few, but one I want to share and help others with is I wish I had known not to drink alcohol and the effect it has on other people and how many people it hurts. The trauma it does to your body and mind. It destroys your dreams, and it takes over your life. You become a person that no one knows, not even "you".

I want them to know that if they "believe" they can overcome this addiction, they can, and God will help them through it. They don't have to handle it alone, because it is too hard to do it by yourself.

I have been sobered for 19 years, and I am going to continue being sober, but I know I have God right there with me. I just wish I had known this a lot sooner, but I know now, and I hope it will help someone not travel that dark road I did.

Chapter

education

Ms. Peterson

Sitting at the bus stop watching the people going by in Memphis, Tennessee, you could see that looking at Ms. Peterson this wasn't the only day this occurred it was a routine it was therapy. She expressed sitting at home makes her depressed.

I wish I had gotten an education to get me through this. I have a tenth-grade education and became pregnant. Now my children are grown, and I am on disability, now I wait on a check month to month. I wish I had known how important an education was and how it would have helped me help myself. I impressed upon my kids the importance of school.

Grace

Grace is a replica of her name, graceful and poise, Ms. Grace is a successful business owner in the beauty industry her business was voted Top Best Massage 2002-07 Graceful Services.

I was introduced to Grace by Joann; they are friends and visiting for the holidays.

Grace was born in Shenzhen, China, but has lived in New York for 20 years Grace had been a nurse taking care of others, so going into the beauty industry was natural.

I wish I had known New York would have given me everything I wanted. I came here looking for happiness and relationship, I got a wonderful husband and a great daughter.

While growing up in China, I was involved in the Cultural Revolution and all education stopped, and I wanted to get a better education. America wants you to create, and I was given the opportunity.

If I had come sooner, the list would be increased of what I would have become. I would have enhanced my relationships with numerous people and my business would have even been better than it is.

Phil

Knowing what I know now, I would have changed my study habits as a child. I always procrastinated with my school, and that made it difficult sometimes to be the best I could in the classroom. My parents (especially my mom) were on me nonstop about my grades, and I appreciate them for that. They did a good job of explaining how important school and education is, and I appreciate them for that.

I wish I had known to take school more seriously and create better study habits, I would know more than I do now. Knowledge is power, and I am always reading something new and exploring new ideas. Who knows how it could have changed my life, but I do know that it would have changed it in a positive. Education is so important. The value of an education is priceless. People think that once you finish high school or college, education is done. But in my opinion, that really is only the beginning. By being more educated than someone, that opens so many new doors that you can explore and the possibilities of endless.

It could only help my relationships. I am not sure how because the relationships I have created over the years are great and only getting better. As time goes, and I learn more, relationships either grow stronger or they start to die off. Education is key, and I believe the more you know, the better circle of friends you will have around you.

Shellie

Shellie hails from Philadelphia she is a dental hygienist, and she loves brightening up smiles.

Shellie replied that she wishes she had known the value of education and continual education. It would have changed my journey, I would have had better decision-making skills, made better choices to get the most out of life. This would have created an increase in wisdom, confidence, career advances and higher income. My relationships would have been stronger, more genuine, and healthier connections.

Mia

Mia is a beautiful woman inside as well as out. She has a heart of gold, we met in school; she was an astute student. Mia is a person that loves to help others.

Mia's response to what she wishes she had known is what a lot of students wish for. Mia says that from the very beginning you have to be concerned about your career path and only accepting jobs that will lead you toward that path and not just taking jobs to get a paycheck. That is what holds people back that have degrees and can't use them, if some way you can work in that field or volunteer the expectations that you will succeed in that field is much greater. I came to this conclusion because I received my degree in Child learning and Development and the level, I think I should be at this time is not where I want to be. I don't have any of the hands-on experience that is needed. If you are going to be a lawyer, find someone to mentor you in that field. Don't be afraid to ask for a job in the law office delivering mail, talk to the attorneys and let them know your plans, someone is going to take you and show you the ropes.

If I had known to take a job in my field and not try to maximize my paycheck. I would be working in my field.

Darren

I wish I had known in early education there was a lack of knowing the different learning styles as we now know from the continuous science of education today. Such pass lack of methods of learning prevented children from believing they could do the work or assignment because of their unique learning style.

It would have helped me be more confident in the different things in education I wanted to explore. I would have enjoyed education more. I wouldn't have just rolled along to get to the next level, I would have examined the subject more in details to help me apply them to my life.

My career choices came from wanting to be an advocate for kids with the same problems I had and excite them about learning and becoming fulfilled with who they are.

Ohio

This nursing student admits he didn't start out putting his best foot forward and wishes he had known nursing school was so hard. I inquired if he had known that would he still pursue that career? The answer was yes, I would have been more serious and paid more attention my freshman year, now I really must work to graduate with honors, but this is what I want to do.

Shashandra

Shasandra immediately answered my question, I wish I had known to think outside the box when entering college and preparing for college and picking majors.

Shanshandra is an awesome young woman who has always been at the top of her class in school and who smiles constantly.

I came from a small town in the Deep South and was not always exposed to many careers or college options. I have always shown appreciation for the people I meet when traveling to other cities, and states. When I would talk to them and find out how prepared people my age was when it came to life options and careers, it made me want to explore more of what I wanted to become. Becoming a lawyer, nurse, teacher, or medical doctor were some of the goals that I dreamed of, and chose because they were challenging and the people who I would meet would be equally energetic and committed as I.

She quickly explained to me that becoming a lawyer, nurse, teacher, or doctor was all that was presented and even though all of those are very admiral careers, but the world is made up of a rainbow of people with different talents and ideas.

Mr. Wheeler

Mr. Wheeler said he wishes he had known to start his master's program earlier, just as other students his last semester of undergraduate just needing a break he decided to wait, and it was harder to make the transition after being out of school for a while. He concluded to start his degree because he was working in the library doing the work, but not getting paid for the level of work he was doing, therefore this led him to continue his education.

It is important for young people to take the risk and even though you may be tired, it is worth the struggle to take the challenge and prepare yourself for the future.

Lois

Lois is a traveling nurse with a great personality and a big smile, we met on the plane and had a wonderful conversation.

Lois said, I would like to pass this information on to the next generation of nurses. When you get to the endocrine system, pay close attention because more than half to eighty percent of your patients in the hospital will be diabetic. I certainly wish I had known.

Anna

Anna got straight to the point when asked the question what you wish you had known.

I wish I had known that grades were so important, I realized that when I started graduate school and I had to pay for it all. If I had done my best, I could have gotten a scholarship to ease the burden on my pocketbook

I wish I had known grades mattered when I realized just how significant my grades were not just to stay in the graduate program, but grades mean money. I had to get loans, and this could have been avoided if I had implemented a better study habit and focused on my grades.

Mat

Mat was born in Houston, Texas, and Matt didn't stray too far from his roots; North Texas is now his home.

I asked him the big questions: what do you wish you had known what would have changed in your life?

Mat said it was a tough question because we all not necessarily regret, but we would have like to have done some things differently not knowing what the outcome would be.

I wish I had known to apply myself in school, although I have been very successful and have had a successful career up to this point, but now I am in a position in my life where I would like to change directions, but because I didn't finish college, because I didn't apply myself very well in junior high and, high school it now limits me to move around in the market-place.

Venice

Venice is from a family of 14 and her parents just wanted her to finish and get a good job. The phrase get a good job is different now. Venice explains I tell my son he can be anything he wants to be, but when I was growing up, finishing high school and getting a good job was the period at the end of the statement. Going to college was certainly a great accomplishment and teaching was the big job to get, that's what women could do. I wanted to be more; engineer something that only men would do at that time, so I wish I had known I could have been anything I wanted to be.

Jose Luis

Hearing Jose's story was uplifting, and I felt so proud of him, knowing his mother was the proudest. How wonderful it was for him to sacrifice to help his family. He was just a teen coming to live with a cousin. Jose stared at 15 washing dishes and then graduating to making salads and pastry. Jose knew he could make more money in New York, so he came and took two jobs not speaking very much English, but he got better. He worked 7 days a week. He was focused on buying his mother a home and his sister that had some health problems not only a home for them, but he had saved and worked hard to return home to Mexico and buy himself a home. The hard work was now a passion of Jose, being a chef and Italian foods is his specialty. His favorite dish is Pancetta carbonara.

His if I had known was, he wishes he had known to get more education to have a better life for his family.

Dr. Vaughn

No matter our accomplishment or our success, there is always something we wish we had known. Dr. Vaughn is a successful surgeon. Growing up in Chattanooga, Tennessee, Bob knew he always wanted to be a doctor and worked hard to get to his goal.

When asked what he wishes he had known, he said, "I wish I had paid more attention in school".

Jordon

I wish I had known to keep in touch with my grade schoolteachers, many of the best ones were a bit older when they taught me and have already passed away. I simply took them for granted when they taught me. Now that I am more mature and a bit wiser, I realize that teaching well is a gift and excellent teachers are blessings to a student. I often feel a loss because I didn't express my gratitude to those teachers who helped me build a solid academic foundation, which has paid dividends for me as a young professional.

Many of my closest friends from college became teachers after graduating. I would have loved to have connected those friends who taught in the Atlanta area to the wonderful teachers I had.

I feel remiss for not sharing my gratitude. As someone who tutored young high school students while in college, I now know how it felt whenever I received a message from a former student saying "hello Jordon" I'm doing well in life and just want to say thanks for helping me years ago. I wish I had known to send similar messages to my great teachers.

Paris

The famous question was asked to Paris and as many, she needed to think about it and then answer, because we all know we need to go through some fields of rocks to get to the yellow brick road.

Paris, in her conservative quiet way, stated: I would not change a lot about my life because everything happened that has happened to me and everything that I have overcame has made and molded me to be who I am today. I do have one regret, which is college. I wish I had known what I wanted to do years ago when I first went to college when I was younger and had all my expenses paid and not a lot of out-of-pocket cost for me. Although I did finish school with a degree in Criminal Justice and a TCC in Early Childhood Education, it wasn't a career choice for me. That forced me to go back twice until I finally found what I liked.

I wasted a lot of time and money. Now that I am older and establish, I now know what I want to do and what I like. I want to move up in my present field. I now need to go back to school with all the credits I have, financial aid is a little more limited and now being married I have more responsibilities, it's harder and more complicated to just go back.

I know if I had known what I wanted to go to school for exactly doors would now be opened, it would have given me more time and experience in my present field (dentistry), and I would have gained a little more financially. I would now be financially stable.

Mary

I wish I had known to start my education earlier. I received my PhD at 57 years old and found out it's hard to build bridges later in life.

Chapter

Relationships

Peng

If I had known what I know now, I would have sought out a mentor. I did things the hard way. I took far longer to accomplish a goal. Furthermore, I did everything alone. I made many mistakes that were not necessary. A mentor would have guided me to avoid silly mistakes. Mistakes others did not make. My parents only had a high school education. Therefore, after I graduated from high school, they did not have the information to guide me. When I started college, I was alone and lost. I had the feeling of what I wanted to accomplish. I did not know what path to take to get there. I did not know how to describe what I wanted to accomplish. I did not know how to organize my thoughts to have a clear vision of my goal.

Most of my life, I worked to repay debt and student loans. I could never move forward or entertain new opportunities as I was always contracted to repay my debt and student loans. I always had to put off or decline opportunities to better myself.

I have stepped away from relationships because I did not know how to balance, choose between the relationship and my family. I did not know how to have my relationship and co excite with my family. I had to do things alone and I choose to do things the hard way. I felt like I was responsible for my family and their wellbeing. I choose not to make a choice and that indecisiveness I lost relationships.

Carol

When entering Alaska Airlines in San Jose, California for my first day on the job, there stood Carol Campanella demeanor of a supervisor, stern and to the point. We ended up being the best of friends, more like mut and jeff I am barely 5 feet, and she is about 6.

Carol was asked the If I had known question.

Carol stated she has taken months and years thinking about the choices she made, and at the time she was going to get married she had a hard time imagining premarital counseling. She thought about how she believed that it was outrageous having someone talk to you and say you are or not compatible but finding out who the other person is takes time. Asking the hard questions that you are afraid to ask and might not be willing to risk. If I had known that making a choice about choosing the wrong partner and father would be such a domino effect watching a lifetime of repercussions this has caused a generation.

Carl

Carl grew up as a military child, traveling the world with his parents. He still loves to travel and most of the time he is with his best friend, his sister. Carl said that as they moved about every two years, the only friend he had immediately was his sister.

I wish I had known how to communicate with women better because I have been engaged twice. If I had known the skill of communications, I would have understood the women better and express how I was feeling, what I expected and what she expected from me, at least one of the engagements could have been salvaged.

AJaye

If I had known previously the relationships, I have been in were toxic I would have gone the other way sooner or never started anything when the red flags on the play were thrown in my face. Relationships have been a major part of what has destroyed my mental health, that I have been working on every day the older I get.

I could typically run down a list of things that I wish I had known and go back and change, but ultimately our lives are already written. It's meant for us to go through what we do because it makes us who we are in the end. From molestation, adoption, rape, losing full custody of my first child, miscarrying another losing my mother, brother and grandfather, losing the one person who was supposed to be there for me regardless of what the situation. Losing friends/associates, I could go on, but each situation has taught me different things and made me stronger. I will continue to grow from every mistake and mishap. With that being said, I would not change a thing. The good Lord knew me in my mother's womb, he knew what I would turn out to be, and without those situations and circumstances I am not sure if I would be the same person that everyone has come to know and love.

Errolyn

Errolyn got right to the point, If I had known how much I loved my husband when I first married him, I would have been a much better wife to him. Now that we have been married for many years now, I know without a doubt that I have been loved, and I am in love with my soul mate.

Sometimes we neglect to see what is right in front of us.

Justin

Justin hails from Pennsylvania, this was a touchy subject, but he wanted to help someone else.

I wish I had known to be a good father, something I didn't have was a good model. My stepfather was a good provider but didn't come outside and play with me and that made it difficult to be the dad I know I should be.

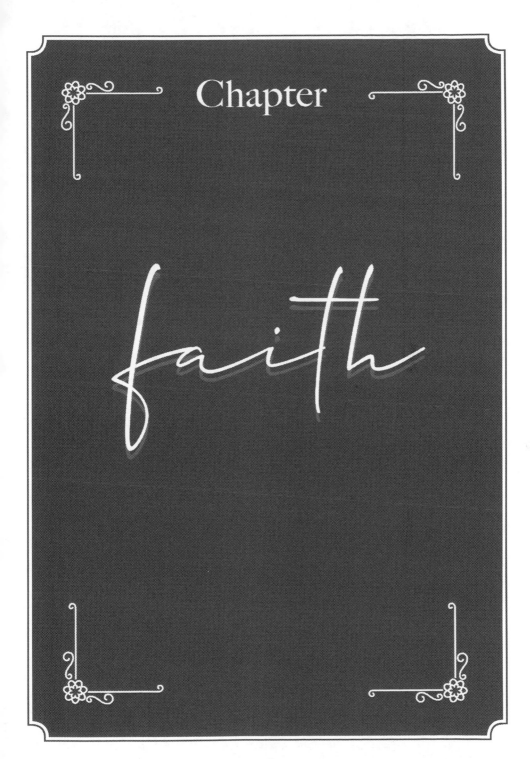

Chapter

faith

Jurgens

On the corners of New York, you will find entrepreneurs of all kinds selling handbags, food hats and gloves and more, but you also see musicians and that lead me to this musician. Jurgens was getting ready to set up for his daily job but what I found out it is a way to survive for Jurgen, who is homeless.

Jurgen is from Germany and has been in New York for 12 years and out on the streets for four of those 12.

Jurgen said he wish he had known to have a deeper relationship with God. Things would have been different. He came to this conclusion as he said it's simple, I understand it more now, I go to church and Bible studies. I was baptized when I was a child, but it didn't mean too much to me then, but now I am a different person.

I play the guitar for survival If I had known more about Jesus it would have created more opportunities. I would have had more peace in my heart and soul in difficult times. My faith wasn't that strong as it is now.

Wanda

If I had known the love of God earlier in my life, it would have been different.

The way I made decisions would have been different, and I know I would have had different outcomes. I would have had a healthy self-esteem.

I started focusing on the Lord in 1986 going to church and reading my Bible.

In 1993, I realized I was free, free to be myself the person God made me to be I was filled with his word and not pretending to be someone that society wanted me to be.

If I Had Known: Wanda

If I had known the love of God earlier in my life, there is no doubt that my life would now be much different.

The way I made my decisions would have been different because I would have had more information to make early decisions with. I would have, to begin with, a higher sense of self-esteem. I was on short term when I should have had a long-term plan.

I started being more focused on the spiritual side of my life and in 1986, I started going to church on a regular basis. Sunday school and on Wednesdays and actually "studying" the Bible. By the time 1993 rolled around, I realized that my thinking had changed. I sensed a form of freedom that was not there previously. I was free to be myself – the person God made me to be. I was filled with His word and even started talking with people, like a minister, and getting them to see how I had changed. It was a change, by the way, that most people had noticed.

Jean

Jean's life in her words was hard as far as her trying to do life's journey on her own and her way. Jean realized that letting go and letting God, she began to feel a sense of peace, success, and love. She no longer feels lonely and feels the love that completes her. Life now for Jean is easier and the journey is not such a maze of difficulty.

Jean stated, if I had known moment was, If I had known how "Good" God was, I would have gotten saved a long time ago.

Tennessee

I wish I had known to have more gratitude. There were times I wanted to quit and give up, but having gratitude created happiness, and I am thankful I listen to my parents, and now I have a career that I love and feels natural, and I am able to give back.

Henry

When you think of Henry Mitchell, you think of numbers and taxes, but when I ask Mr. Mitchell who is from Liberia, what he wished he had known are these:

I wish I had known to take God for whom/what he is, not for who/what he is not. How might that have changed your life, your journey?

The journey could have been more focused and directional since God's word, as I know it today, could have guided me in making the right choices such as choosing a life partner and friends.

Every life decision-making ought to have God as the key parameter, since God knows tomorrow, not man. New opportunities abound when decision-making is made with God as the pivot.

Knowing God, for whom/what he is, enhances relationships and that is why I believe I should have put God first, knowing what I know now.

Tytiana

Tytiana is an aspiring actor, we talked about her career, and about life as a young person today. She admits there are differences today compared to her parents, but one thing we both agreed that each generation has its own obstacles to overcome.

I wish she had known that my parents knew more than I did and listening to them would have made, my life easier.

As I gets older, I thank God for bringing me through the obstacles I have presented to myself even the mistakes I have made, God has seen me through and has put a lot of positive people in my path. Being young is fun, but being careful about the choices you make in life is so important because the choices you make will catch up with you.

Melvin

Melvin is a man of few words, but when he speaks, it is of substance. When asked what he wish he had known, it was immediate and of substance. Melvin said knowing what I know now, he wishes he had known God, wanting to serve him and follow him earlier.

This would have created new opportunities that when God was opening up doors of opportunities I would see and understand them as I do now. Being close to God would have increased my faith.

Ms. Howard

Ms. Howard is a very poised, but strong businesswoman that has had 85 years of learning and teaching life and helping others that have been mistreated. This is brought on by the mistreatment in her own life.

Ms. Howard said If I had known, I could have gone to college to be a designer. I wanted to design costumes for the movies, but I didn't have the faith I needed. I wanted to depend on my mother. Unaware at the time that God was the one in charge. My mother didn't help.

I didn't have faith in the Lord and myself to get the task done. My faith was ruined, and I went to college for accounting. I now know that God is the one I need to ask for anything and everything.

Vanessa

I would have focused more in school, and built my confidence, so I would have had better self-esteem.

I would have been around more friends that had a positive attitude in life and wanted to achieve more in life.

My life still came out amazing, "thanks to God". I left home for the (U.S. Army) military immediately after graduating from high school because I knew I could not afford college. My journey in life changed. The military gave me a new opportunity. I found new positive friends, I got back my relationship with God, and through it all God brought me a soul mate. I have now been married for 39 years.

Life is a journey; you need to know what journey God has you on.

Allow God to be first in your life and let him lead the way.

Your journey will be a lot easier.

Kym

I have never been asked this question before, so bear with me. I think most people, including myself, would have tons to change. I have reflected on this, and I believe that if I would have changed the difficult and trying times it would have not made me who I am today. I want to say nothing, but I have one big If I had known that I will share.

I do wish I had known one thing which would have changed me to the positive sooner is what I have experience in the last two years. I believe new opportunities have been created in abundance for me in the past 2 years. Why in the last 2 years? I have built a relationship with God and continued to grow in faith, prayer, and the word. As this wonderful part of my life has opened, I have been blessed. I have found purpose in my life and when I did my current relationships became stronger. God placed new people and relationships in my life that has touched my life greatly.

Adam

Adam is a former firefighter and now has a job that is more comfortable for his family to live with and enjoy his arrival coming home. He is a very proud father and says he has three perfect kids.

Adam was very specific in his answer of what he wishes he had known If I had known the best way to make others happy was to make myself happy. I wish I had known to do that.

I wish I had looked out for my needs and been true to myself when I was younger, and I wish I had known I didn't need validation from others, only from God. I wish I had known to fear God not man, I would have sought out the plan that God wanted me to follow.

Liam

I wish I had known that I needed to live a life of purpose for Christ and to help others, impacting their lives for their betterment. I found out trying drugs, women, and music emptiness still prevailed, so I became a missionary, and my life was fulfilled.

London England

I had such a positive experience in London, with the people we encountered. As our granddaughter says, they were so kind. We ask for directions, and they stopped and took us to the stop and waited until we were on the trolley safely.

I ask the young lady what she wishes she had known, and immediately she said she wishes she would have known everything would turn out alright. I guess we all need a little more faith.

Lynn

I wish I had known I was important enough; I am going through a lot of trials. God is revealing to me, if I just ask him, he will give me what I need. If I had known this earlier, I would be a lot further and happier.

Minsk Belarus

I ask this gentleman where he was from, and he told me Minsk, Belarus, which is close to Ukraine. The conversation continued with the famous question what do you wish you had known?

He thought for a moment, and it was like a light bulb lit up. I wish I had known not to worry so much; they will work themselves out. If I had known this, I would not have had so much stress, and it makes your work harder if you worry about everything.

Oakland California

If I had known what my life would have been like for 10 years. I would have never dated the guy I married. I changed my life around and got back in the same life I had left. I was living in the world, doing things I should not have done. When I decided to change my life around, my husband was not willing to change. I went to a homeless shelter and told him to get his life in order. I told him that God would move him out of my way and put somebody else in his place. It was nobody but God, I met a man that changed my life, I dated him for 6 months and married him, and we've been together ever since.

Peter

How do you love someone that you have seen beat your parents and other family members, kill and deceive your people. Peter is from Rhodesia before it was Zimbabwe; all he saw was ill-treatment and segregation and wanted revenge.

Well, when I ask Peter what you wish you had known, he said he wish he had known God earlier. A college friend invited him to a church event, and he gave his testimony. He told him about what God had done for him and his life was so much like his, so when the Gospel was preached it was like a letter describing his life. He was inspired and was released from the hatred and bitterness that was bottled up inside and immediately all the sickness was released from his body stomach ulcers, and he had freedom. I have peace in the mist of the storm, I know God is in control.

Tabitha

Some people you meet, and they feel like family, that's exactly what happened with Tabitha. I was so amazed at her wisdom at such a young age and her respect for others older and younger. We talked, and it was if I was talking to a family member. I am so grateful to have her in my life.

I ask her what she wished she had known; it didn't take her long to answer, in fact she had an answer ready as if she had been waiting for this moment.

Tabitha

I wish I had known to make it my business to build my relationship with God and myself first. Which should have happened, but wasn't the case for me, but I am happy I know now that God is so amazing!

This would have changed my life because my foundation would have been solid, and every move would have been based off God's love and standards. It would have kept me from a lot of pain and hurt. It would have allowed me to prosper and flourish in a different light. My relationships would have enhanced on every level based on love and no hurt. When you come from a place of hurt, you tend to hold back on things you do, and you can miss your blessings.

I am thankful for all the lessons I have learned and experienced because without them, I would not be where I am today and would not have met your beautiful spirit to have you as an additional auntie.

Vivian

Vivian and I met at church, and she was writing her own book "From Dreams to Awakening"

She had a story to tell me just as soon as I ask the question. I laughed at first and then she went into depth, and it wasn't funny, but what I had done also just maybe in a differently, but I will let her explain.

If I had known and understood that Father knows best, I would have listened to his words even when it was not in agreement with my agenda.

As a five-year-old, I stubbornly refused when my dad said I had to go to school. Each day I would make an attempt to miss the bus. Each day he would swipe my hiney until I got on the bus. Eventually I surrendered and started getting on the bus. Today I'd like to think I realized I was fighting a losing battle. In attending wholeheartedly, I soon found that I really did like learning new things, especially reading and writing. I wish I had known!

By the same token, when I began to feel like I wanted to spend the rest of my life with the man I had chosen, I ask God for guidance. In reply, God said: Do not be yoked together with unbelievers. For what do righteousness and wickedness have in common? Or what fellowship can light have with darkness? What harmony is there between Christ and Belial? Or what does a believer have in common with an unbeliever?

What agreement is there between the temple of God and idols? For we are the temple of the living God.

2 cor6:14-16 NIV Warning against idolatry

It wasn't the answer I was looking for, so I disregarded the guidance. Instead, I went the way of Baalim, kept going back to God until I thought he changed his mind and said it's better to marry than to burn.

Today I know that God, being the gentleman he is, was not going to override the free will he had given me. God changes not. The swiping I got from my earthly father are a drop in the bucket in comparison with the consequences of my disobedience to my Heavenly Father. I have come truly to recognize that all choices come with consequences. Good choices yield good consequences, bad choices yield bad consequences.

If I had known and learned that lesson when my father tried to teach it to me, just maybe I could have avoided the high cost of disobedience to my Heavenly Father.

I conclude by saying insight avoids unnecessary hardships, thus If I had Known!

Hindsight, when allowed to speak, learns from those painful negative experiences only after entering the arena. In the midst of the consequences, I realized it was pastime to listen and take heed.

Now I know Father does know best, and it is my hope other people who are reading this will learn from my mistakes and be saved from what for me have been many years of reckoning.

Brenda

In my life what I would have done differently and wish I had known was to tell more people about God's overwhelming love.

This would have created new opportunities for me because it would have been the dynamite of my life. This would have enhanced my relationships because with the love God gives to me I would love people more, giving them what they needed most in life to become the best they could be by sharing God's love.

I wish I had known how amazing his love was and is, nothing compares to his love.

Velma

If I had known about God's love, I would have prayed, waited, and seek God's guidance on his plan for my life. I would have trusted that all circumstances good and bad was an opportunity for the work of God to be displayed in my life. I would not have thought I was being punished or that I am not good enough, or no one loves me. I thank God in spite of myself he has blessed me abundantly.

I would have dreamed bigger, been more confident, would have made better relationship choices. I would have saved myself many sleepless nights and I would have cried tears of joy for all God was doing in my life, rather than tears of disappointments, shame fear and discontentment. The opportunities God has for me probably took a lot longer because I stood in the way of God's blessings. I probably missed out on some what might have been.

If I had known I would have been more committed, less judgmental, and self-assured that God got me in all conditions. I can be fearless and dare to be great.

I thank God I now know to wait on the Lord and know he has a better plan. Trust him!

Chapter

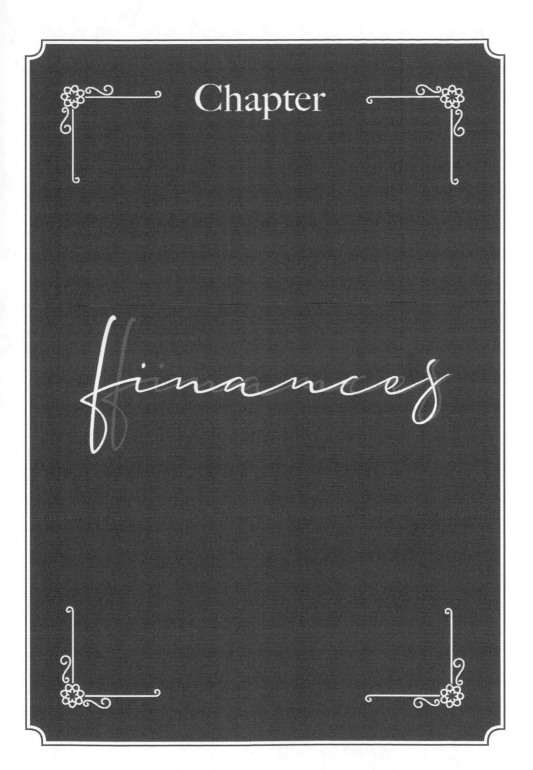

finances

Pastor Elmore

As I have learned throughout life, you need every struggle to make you stronger. I am truly one that embraces the journey and understands the structural order of process. However, if I could change anything about my life and if I had known, I would have delayed my gratification a lot more. As a young man I made hundreds of thousands of dollars and just as fast as I earned them, I spent them! I did not have a vision for ownership in my life. Coming from a household that did not speak about credit or teach about financial literacy, it placed me in a broke mindset with a lot of money. If I could take it from the top, I would save more, invest more, and use more wisdom financially to better position my family legacy. The Bible says that it's my job to leave a blessing for my children's children!

I would be more financially stable now. I took the long road to financial peace. I had to fight harder because of my early decisions.

This would have created new opportunities for me. I would have more investment capital by now to be able to effectively do stronger ministry. As a church, it's best that pastors are able to invest in their mission. I believe we do very well, but we could do much better, and I've been in a better financial position earlier in life.

Relationships would've been enhanced for the simple fact that when people around you are not broke, they are happier. I'm a firm believer that you attract who you are.

Texas

I wish I had known about credit, how to build it and how to prevent it from taking you down the wrong path and enslaving you for life.

I wish I would have known, so I could have taught my kids, which would have helped them from getting into debt.

If I had known the truth and strategies of money, and credit, my wife and I would not have struggled for eight years.

Maggie

If you want to know anything about a cat, ask Maggie. She can tell you what kind of cat, when he or she should eat and diagnose the problems. Maggie is at her best and has a glow on her face when talking about Cats. Maggie also rescues cats.

Maggie responded to the question of If I had known.....

I live day by day, so I wish I had known how to make more money, I wish I had known how to value myself worth.

I never set a goal, just lived one day at a time, and had no recipe.

Dr. Young

Dr. Young alongside his beautiful wife Sonya has a beautiful marriage and family, very successful business, and dental practice for 63 years. There was an if I had known, even though he started dental clinics overseas and mentored many young people and helped them either find their purpose or turn their lives around at the Andrew and Walter Young YMCA and served in the military.

When ask what he wishes he had known, he immediately answered. I wish I had known, more about finances, credit, stocks, and money overall. I wish I had been taught this early in my professional life, it would have helped me in my business and my home.

Dr. Swanson

If you hate going to the dentist, here is a chance to find a calm, caring and gentle dentist. Comments from the patients that he service says he goes the extra mile to make sure you have a big smile every day.

Dr. Swanson stated he wished he had known about money, how it worked, at an early age. How not to trade time for money. I was never taught in school about investing. I didn't know in the beginning I could own a business and to stay away from debt, which keeps you in bondage. I know this would have changed my life and changed the way I would have taught my children. I always heard and was taught to go to school, get a good job and work until retirement.

I now want to take the opportunity to expose my children and grandchildren to everything about finances, so that they will know the world is much bigger than what's in front of them. I want them to learn how to work smarter, not harder, spending every minute trying to make a dollar. I want them and every young person to know what I wish I had known.

Lyndon

I met Lyndon about 20 years ago in a restaurant, he's like a son and part of the family.

Lyndon stated he wishes he had known to spend more time at a younger age to understand my culture and what my roots truly are. It would have changed my perspective on life, what I value, the person I chose to build my life with and my expectations of myself.

This would have helped me create new opportunities in helping others and giving back because I would understand more thoroughly.

It would have enhanced my relationships when meeting people with different experiences than mine and opening my eyes to someone else's journey and path.

Coming from a not-so-great area of town and not having the best examples growing up. If I had known to invest at an earlier age, what credit meant to your likeness and how being responsible carries over into many other parts of your life, I feel like I would have benefited tremendously earlier in life.

Tonya

Tonya is a beautiful lady, served in the military and is a wonderful wife and mother to three awesome children. Tonya gleams when she talks about her husband and children. I met her on a mission trip, and so many similarities were discussed.

Tonya stated that she wishes she had known more about and the benefit of compound interest. I would have bought our first home a lot sooner. Although I bought it before age 30, I would have accumulated wealth a lot sooner. The Bible says, "A good man leaves an inheritance to his children's children, but the wealth of the sinner is stored up for the righteous" Proverbs 13:22.

It was always expected of me to be a Christian, a good citizen and get a good job, that's what I was always taught as a child. Had more emphasis been placed on accumulating wealth, I believe opportunities for my family, and I would have materialized much sooner. I'm truly grateful for the journey because God showed me how to depend on him only.

I believe my journey would have been a lot smoother in acquiring things. I would have established credit through homeownership that would have given me the ability to pursue venture capital moves an entrepreneur a lot sooner.

The paths and places I've visited has afforded me to see and meet a diverse group of people in my life. Serving in the Military started that journey of discovery as God allowed me to appreciate differences in cultures. God furthered my journey after the military in building my character by blessing me with a career that led me all over the world. Experiencing first-hand what you read about sharing or see in movies is humbling when sharing with others. I believe at times most of my relationships were sparked out of curiosity. My friends shared during my travels, which lead to hours of long conversations. However, the fortunes God had afforded me attracted the attention and relationships of extended family and friends, at times were challenging out of jealousy.

Chapter

Time

Breshena

We get in the habit of living the Friday-to-Friday life and even have the slogan, "Thank God It's Friday," which speaks volumes about how we deplore the workweek and all that takes place during that period. We tend to forget the importance and the previous moments we all miss because of the hustle and bustle of everyday struggle of climbing the imaginary (in our minds it's real) ladder to "success" in whatever it is we are aiming for. Examining sickness and tragedies, you immediately know that you need to stop and smell the roses, you take long walks and enjoy the scenery, forgive, and know that you cannot continue to sweat the small stuff.

Breshena exclaims that getting older will make you wish you had known how important and precious time is. Looking back at pictures.

If I had known what I know now, and say, ten years ago, I am sure that I would be much further along than I am now. When you learn a lot, you realize that it's time to get serious with life. I wish I had known how precious time is.

Iran

———◦❦◦———

I wish I had known surgery would be as hard as it is. It is very time-consuming and it makes me realize how important time is and how very precious it is.

Saudi Arabia

This young medical student talk to me about two things he wishes he had known.

I wish I had known to read certain books and spent more time with friends, and wish I had known about the gift of time.

Chapter

choices

Aaron

I met Aaron at a store a few months back and as I talked to him, I wondered as a young man. What he wished he had known something and if anything he thought he had known would have made his life better. His answers surprised me because still as a young man he had realized what he had done and could now try to change it.

Aaron told me that while growing up he was advanced in education but fell prey to peer pressure and ventured off the track.

Aaron's college experience was harder because he stopped stimulating his mind and his level of knowledge decreased.

Aaron responded and said I wish I had known the consequences of my actions as a youth affected me now as an adult. I know my life would have been much easier.

Jennifer

I wish I had known that my parents were right about life and not undermine their intelligence. I probably would have had a completely different life. My life thus far has been good, but certain struggles made me stagnant for periods of time. My mother and father had the approach of we will guide you, give you advice and support. However, when in your late teens, early twenties you tend to think the world revolves around you. I'm sure I would have graduated from college at least have my master's degree, but I chose a path of I can do whatever I want. With my knowledge now, taking the hard road, I appreciate the trials and tribulations, but I still wish I had just taken maybe an ounce of their wisdom.

Derryl

I would be married by now if I had known that I wasn't always right and things didn't have to go my way all the time, and that compromise was my best friend.

I wish I had paid attention to my inter voice about the women I met. I have met some amazing women and should have realized the importance of them emotionally and psychologically and most of all understand the love they were giving me.

I have come to this conclusion because I am still single and realized that I let my great women get away, and I didn't have to be a single father.

Furthermore, I would be married by now if I had known the importance of forming a relationship.

Elaine

It's wonderful when you recognize at an early age that what you're doing or going to school for is not what is going to make you happy.

I met this young lady Elaine, she stated some of us have been told to go to school for certain things some of us have a vision of what we think a job is and find out that it is not what we want to do every day, I was going to school and was told you do A plus B plus C, and you'll be happy. I found out that is not always what makes you happy. Elaine said she wishes she had known there was no right way to one path in life, everyone's journey is unique.

Dionica

Dionica is from the Dominican Republic has been in New York for 17 years and works at a well-known hotel in New York, so she was very friendly, but was very adamant about she was on duty, so no pictures could be taken, and her work needed to continue. As she worked, she politely answered my question with a few minutes of thought.

I wish I had known to follow my own dreams and not my ex-husband. I love math and wish to teach math. I look at others that have gone on to fulfill their dreams. I am hesitant but considering going back to school, maybe online because I am so thankful for this job.

Geofry

Sitting at a table trying to get a quick bite before the masses come in. Geofry was nice enough to talk to me and give me his views of What he wishes he had known.

Geofry is from Nigeria and wanted to be a Dis Jockey or music producer that would have made him happy to sit in classes and interpret music or just listen to it would be the best, but where he is from that is not an acceptable degree you are to become a lawyer doctor are the most respectable careers.

Geofry has been a restaurant manager for 23 years and have been with this well-known bakery for 13 years. It happened to be one of my favorites that I loved to frequent after church.

I know music would have changed my path.

Juan

Juan always has a smile on his face, even when asked what do you wish you had known?

His reply I wish I would have known to do what I wanted to do instead of having a woman give me an ultimatum saying she would leave me if I left, and she ended up leaving anyway.

I want to go to school and go to the military I started going to school and was in a bad accident, and now I am planning to go back to school, but I wish I had done it earlier.

Terry

Terry is a 57-year-old female, and if I had known that her time that she worked the city as a surveyor and her time now with the post office could have given her a nice and early retirement.

What I want young girls to know is that the money I took from the retirement that I received from the city I took and used it to help my ex-husband buy a truck and that didn't work out, so Terry said, "Girls don't take your money to buy a man".

Patricia

I met this vibrant young lady in the Atlanta airport, she had a very pleasing personality and willing to share her ideas and answer my question. Patricia is a Chicagoan, an author, and an entrepreneur.

Patricia said if I wish I had known what I know now, I would have completed college when I was 18 and majored in nursing.

I would have stayed in the army when I got pregnant with my first son.

Doc

Doc had a very bad childhood with an alcoholic mother, and the pendulum could have swung either direction. He could have chosen to be an alcoholic, or he could have done just what he did. Doc decided to excel and become the best he could be. He felt if he could do good in school elementary, high school he could get into college and if he did well in college he could get into medical school, and he did just that. Great student, great husband, great father and great doctor.

Doc answered the question of If I had known that I needed to confront my mother about her parenting or lack of. If I had known that doing this would have alleviated a tremendous amount of stress from my life growing up it is too late now, she has since passed away, and I still have unresolved answers.

Allison

I ask Allison what you wish you had known, she said:

I wish I would have known how much regret I would have had knowing I put off my dreams and waiting and doing what someone else wanting me to do.

When I took my life, back I did what I wanted to do, and I am now happy.

Laura

I wish I had known to invest in myself instead of so many others. After I retired, I found out I needed to take care of me.

Kandy

I wish I had known that if I had stayed on campus longer than 2 years and wait to declare my major in college after my first 2 years, I wouldn't have been so financially stressed. The toll of moving into an apartment and needing to work two jobs. I worked my entire college career except for one semester, and that also doubled the time it took me to graduate. I had to be a full-time employee to pay bills and a part-time student. I would have been out of school on time, therefore making me feel so behind. I became a high functioning/hyper independent woman to try to make up the time.

I would have been less stressed and anxious around certain people in my life/family if I had not always felt like I was chasing my tail and trying to make up for lost time being in school and working 2 jobs. If I had known the above, I could have visited home more and would have been able to mend relationships that needed it sooner.

Jocelyn:

Kandy brings to light what a lot of young people face after going off to college, wanting to be on their own and not being aware of the financial burdens that comes with it if you are not prepared. Time passes so much faster when you align yourself with the process.

Kaleb

Kaleb is a 17-year-old senior in high school and did not ponder when I explained to him what I was asking.

Kaleb: I was in the eighth grade, selecting my electives for high school. I selected the first thing that I saw, not really taking this choice serious. I selected mechanics also called automotive repair. When school started, and I was in the ninth grade, I realized I had made a big mistake. I had no interest in the class I had selected; I didn't even have an interest in cars. I later found out I could have taken a class I was interested in, digital technology.

We were given a personality test, and this would have helped me tremendously, it would have had an impact on my decision-making, my life and making a choice for my classes with passion and concern. The semester was unproductive, although I did pass. It would have changed my life because I would have been able to take dual enrollment college courses. I would have already started credits for my career.

I wish I had known that you need to take things seriously no matter what the degree of the choice, because it may affect your life for a short period of time, or it just may affect it for a lifetime. I will give each decision more thought of what and how it will impact my life.

LaTonya

I wish I had known the effects of getting pregnant at an early age, which interrupted me pursuing my passion to becoming a nurse.

My life might have changed in me getting my career first, marriage and then children. Having a career at 23 could have opened more doors. Becoming more knowledgeable about homeownership, finances, and retirement to a place where now at my age I could be sharing good news to people all over the world. Maturity, having wisdom can make you a better person, friend, sister, brother, wife, and mother I think, especially with age.

Wisdom implies a breath of knowledge and a depth of understanding. Those who are wise treasure up knowledge, but the mouth of the fool invites ruin. Proverbs 10:14

It has been an honor and a pleasure to meet
all of you and to learn from you!

Thank You

Printed in the United States
by Baker & Taylor Publisher Services